<u>Rightly Dividing The Word</u>

Philippians Verse by Verse

A Reformed Bible Study for Women

ISBN 978-1-4303-0443-2

Introduction

Welcome to our study on Philippians verse by verse!

You will need a Bible in hand for this study, as many times only parts of verses will be quoted in our commentary. Verses quoted are in *italic* print along with their reference numbers.

Most of the Scripture used in this study is the New American Standard Updated Edition, as it relays the English counterparts of the Greek and Hebrew words well. Feel free to use the translation you are most comfortable with. Any formal translation will benefit you greatly.

Our study is divided into four weeks. We will spend one week on each chapter of Philippians. Every week we will have five days of lessons plus an additional 'Weekend Stop'.

Lastly, when you see our thoughtful little friend shown to the left, we will stop and ponder together for a moment. Sometimes there will be questions or, sometimes just a thought that has the potential to change our life direction. Please do take the time to ponder and think on each of God's precious verses, whether our little friend is present or not, it will surely be a good use of your time. May God richly bless you for taking time to study His Word. I am looking forward to our journey together. Let's get started!

Week One

<u>Day One</u>

1:1 *[From] Paul and Timothy, bond-servants of Christ Jesus....*

Paul begins by identifying himself and his companion to the readers. And, of all the things Paul could say about himself, he says, "From Paul... a bond-servant of Christ Jesus." This is his identity. Not a Pharisee, a rabbi, not an equivalent of a TH.D. in his day, not *Dr. Paul to* ... simply, Paul: a servant of Christ Jesus.

How many times in life our identity comes from what we do, such as: "I am an engineer," or, "I am Julie's mom," or, "I put together the church bulletins." But what it really boils down to is who we are in Christ.

Let's look at the word 'bond servant'.
A <u>bond-servant</u> is someone who is devoted to, even consumed with another to the disregard of one's own interests. This can be a voluntary or involuntary servanthood.

Are we too, devoted, even consumed with Christ's will even to the disregard of our own fleshly desires?

_____

_____

_____

_____

_____

_____

_____

Where does your identity come from? Where should it come from?

_____

_____

_____

_____

_____

_____

_____

_____

_____

_____

_____

_____

_____

_____

_____

~~~

1:2 *Grace to you and peace from God our Father and the Lord Jesus Christ.*

I just LOVE this greeting, don't you?! Paul uses it in some form or fashion in all of his epistles. *Grace* expresses God's love to His elect, and peace expresses the result of partaking of God's grace!

1:3 *I thank my God....*

Paul thanks God each time he remembers his Christian brothers and sisters. What an example for us to do the same thing! In the spaces below, list some brothers and sisters in

Christ that you are thankful for. Try to remember them in your prayers tonight.

_____

_____

_____

_____

_____

_____

_____

_____

~~~

1:4 *always offering prayer with joy in my every prayer for you all, in view of your participation in the gospel from the first day until now*

Wow! With your pen circle the words 'always' and 'every'. Underline the word 'joy'. Now re-read the text. See how strongly Paul wrote this? He is filled with overflowing joy at the participation of the Philippian church in God's work. He states that EVERY prayer for them was filled with joy, and he always offered up the prayers! Glory! And, he remembered them through so many circumstances: in Thessalonica (Philippians 4:15.), in Corinth (Acts 18:5; 2 Corinthians 11:7-10), and now in Rome.

This was a church that helped support Paul.

Consider the importance of our support to brothers and sisters doing the work of Christ both at home and abroad.

~~~

<u>Day Two</u>

1:5-6 *...being confident of this, that he who began a good work in you will carry it on to completion until the day of Christ Jesus* (NIV)

What a reassuring verse! There are many places in Paul's epistles where he states this. In 1 Corinthians 1:8, Paul writes, *[God] who will also confirm you to the end, blameless in the day of our Lord Jesus Christ.*

1 Thessalonians 5:23-24 states, *Now may the God of peace Himself sanctify you entirely; and may your spirit and soul and body be preserved complete, without blame at the coming of our Lord Jesus Christ. Faithful is He who calls you, and He also will bring it to pass.*

There are so many more verses like this, but for the sake of our study time, we will limit ourselves to these right now.

A common teaching in many churches is that any individual person can "mess up" the plan God has for their lives, and make God go to a "plan b"...and "c", and "d"... Is that what these verses teach? Why or why not?

_____

_____

_____

_____

_____

_____

_____

_____

_____

_____

_____

_____

_____

No. Scripture teaches the very opposite of mankind 'foiling' God's plan for them. It teaches that God's sovereign will shall be done despite our shortcomings!

The next argument to God's sovereignty over man is "but man can sin, and therefore spoil what work God was doing."

Let us look at what Scripture has to say about this argument.

Genesis 4:7 *If you do well, will not your countenance be lifted up? And if you do not do well, sin is crouching at the door; and its desire is for you, but you must master it.*

1 Corinthians 9:26-27 *Therefore I run in such a way, as not without aim; I box in such a way, as not beating the air; but I discipline my body and make it my slave, so that, after I have preached to others, I myself will not be disqualified*

Romans 6:23 *For the wages of sin is death, but the free gift of God is eternal life in Christ Jesus our Lord*

Please take a moment to read what Hebrews 12:4-13 says about God's discipline shown to those He loves. God will teach His children, guide His children and discipline His children both temporally and when we stand before Christ and are judged. Sometimes we are judged by God immediately for our sin, sometimes the judgment tarries (1 Timothy 5:24), but God <u>corrects</u> our behavior rather than being foiled by our behavior.

Your thoughts and insights:

_____

_____

_____

_____

_____

_____

_____

_____

_____

It is He that is God, and we His creation. The Creator will not be foiled by the creation, nor will the potter by the clay.

~~~

1:7-8 *For it is only right for me to feel this way about you all, because I have you in my heart....*

Notice Paul does not write that he feels this way about the Philippians because "God commanded him" or "because he has to" but he writes with affection. We too should show each other the same grace and affection in Christ. In verse eight, he restates the statement more strongly, "*For God is my witness, how I long for you all with the affection of Christ Jesus*"

How often do you see this attitude in the church today? How can we change our behavior so there is one more voice that reflects the spirit of the Scriptures?

_____

_____

_____

_____

_____

_____

~~~

1:9-11 And this I pray, that your love may abound still more and more in real knowledge and all discernment, so that you may approve the things that are excellent, in order to be sincere and blameless until the day of Christ; having been filled with the fruit of righteousness which comes through Jesus Christ, to the glory and praise of God.

Wow! What a powerful prayer? Don't you love it? This is a prayer I've prayed for myself and for my husband many, many years. Let's take a minute and break it down.

a) And this I pray, that your love may abound still more and more in real knowledge and all discernment

What trait does Paul list first? _____

Do you think this is consistent with his writing in 1 Corinthians 13:13 *But now faith, hope, love, abide these three; but the greatest of these is love?* _____

Next Paul prays for real knowledge and discernment. Notice how Paul feels it is important to couple even knowledge of God and His ways with love.

b) so that you may approve the things that are excellent, in order to be sincere and blameless until the day of Christ

Notice Paul wants them to test and prove not only good things, but the very best things. Things of superior excellence may not be so easily discerned, except by the mature Christian.

The writer of Hebrews states, *For everyone who partakes only of milk is not accustomed to the word of righteousness, for he is an infant. But solid food is for the mature, who because of practice have their senses trained to discern good and evil.* (Hebrews 5:13-14)

These verses speak of two things: 1) Knowing God and His Word and 2) practicing the principles (training the senses). No matter how great the Christian's walk is, no matter how 'righteous' and upright we are, we can all improve on one or more of these areas. Can you identify one of these areas in your life that you can commit to working on?

c) *having been filled with the fruit of righteousness which comes through Jesus Christ, to the glory and praise of God*

One of the fruits of the Spirit is righteousness –
not our own, but our righteousness in Christ,
and our change of will, from seeking our own
desires to seeking His and longing to please
Him.

~~~

<u>Day Three</u>

1:12-14 *Now I want you to know, brethren, that my circumstances have turned out for the greater progress of the gospel.... most of the brethren, trusting in the Lord because of my imprisonment, have far more courage to speak the word of God without fear*

Read Philippians 4:8 below. Paul really practices what he preaches doesn't he?!

Finally, brethren, whatever is true, whatever is honorable, whatever is right, whatever is pure, whatever is lovely, whatever is of good repute, if there is any excellence and if anything worthy of praise, dwell on these things

How do you think our lives would change if we practiced these principles?

_____

_____

_____

_____

_____

Read Proverbs 23:7. What does it say about
what a man thinks?

_____

_____

_____

_____

_____

Look up Luke 6:45. What does it say the
mouth speaks from?

_____

_____

_____

_____

If we dwell on something, don't you think that
is what will fill our heart? So often I catch
myself dwelling on the negative and fearful.
That fills my heart and then I voice it. How
much freer we could be living if we could just

practice the Biblical principal of "counting our blessings!"

~~~

1:15-18 *Some, to be sure, are preaching Christ even from envy and strife....thinking to cause me distress in my imprisonment What then? Only that in every way, whether in pretense or in truth, Christ is proclaimed; and in this I rejoice. Yes, and I will rejoice*

In context, Paul was a prisoner in Rome and spoke of those who mocked him and his gospel by preaching it out of envy and strife with harmful intent, as well as those who preached it out of love. Paul states that either way, Christ is preached and in this he rejoices.

Bringing it home: List all the different Christian denominations you can on the lines below. Don't spend more than two minutes on this part of the activity. I bet you will run out of lines before you run out of time!

1._____

2._____

3._____

4._____

5._____

6._____

7._____

8._____

9._____

10_____

11._____

12._____

13._____

14._____

15._____

There are some things worth separating from a denomination over. I would look for another denomination if mine did not believe and preach in the sovereignty and authority of God, that Christ walked the earth both fully man and fully God, and that the only way to salvation was through faith in Christ's atoning work to name just a few things. These are core issues that cannot be compromised. Yet, there are many different denominations that have the same core values but practice their worship differently. Our society has a habit of thinking that one denomination (usually the one they are part of) is better and much more godly than that heathen _____(fill in the blank with another denomination name) denomination. You do not have to look long and hard to hear that one denomination knows that IT is going to heaven, but "this other one...well....."

This is not the example Paul gives us in his own writing and attitude. To repeat his words, "*What then? Only that in every way, whether in pretense or in truth, Christ is proclaimed; and in this I rejoice. Yes, and I will rejoice*"

We will have to examine the next verse to find out why Paul will rejoice no matter the circumstances that surround the preaching of Christ.

~~~

<u>Day Four</u>

1:19-20 *for I know that this will turn out for my deliverance through your prayers and the provision of the Spirit of Jesus Christ, according to my earnest expectation and hope, that I will not be put to shame in anything, but that with all boldness, Christ will even now, as always, be exalted in my body, whether by life or by death*

Ah, Paul brings it back to both a personal note, as well as re-affirming the character of God. He states that no matter what happens, Christ will be *exalted* [Greek for *exalted*: glorified, made great, esteemed] by life or death. That is, no matter what happens to Paul, God will have orchestrated it to His own glory. Paul reaffirms the sovereignty of God.

I think if I were in Paul's shoes, it would be easy to wonder if because I had "messed up" that I landed in prison again. Then I might wonder, "If I have not messed up why would God allow me to be in prison?" I would wonder how much greater my ministry for him would be if I was free.

Would you wonder the same thing? Yet, these are not Biblical thoughts sisters. In hindsight, we can see that Paul's ministry reached far more people for far more generations than if he had not written a word on paper because he was free to travel.

Let us take a moment and ponder the things in our life right now that we do not think are going smoothly, or are wondering how God can allow it. Write them on the lines below, then like Paul, let us give them to God, knowing He will use all things for His glory. *And we know that God causes all things to work together for good to those who love God, to those who are called according to His purpose* (Romans 8:28) Remember, what is ultimately for our good, may not seem pleasant at the moment!

_____

_____

_____

_____

_____

_____

_____

_____

_____

~~~

1:21 *For to me, to live is Christ and to die is gain.*

This is one of the most famous verses in the Bible. Don't you think? Yet, this is so rich. It is the call of our own lives too. Christ calls us to die to self and to live for Him. Look up the following verses and paraphrase them on the lines below using your own words.

Romans 8:12-14

_____

_____

_____

_____

_____

_____

_____

_____

Colossians 3:3

_____

_____

_____

_____

_____

Galatians 2:20

_____

_____

_____

_____

_____

Romans 12:1

_____

_____

_____

_____

_____

_____

According to these verses, how are we supposed to live our lives? And, for whom are we supposed to live our lives?

_____

_____

_____

_____

_____

_____

_____

_____

~~~

Day Five

1:22 *But if I am to live on in the flesh, this will mean fruitful labor for me; and I do not know which to choose*

Paul longs to be with His Lord, clothed with his heavenly body, yet he understands that if he is to live longer here on earth, the fruit of his living longer, is that he can labor more.

Despite the hardships of our own daily life, despite the goals we set for ourselves, do we also long to labor for the Lord?

~~~

1:23-26 *But I am hard-pressed from both directions...yet to remain on in the flesh is more necessary for your sake. Convinced of this, I know that I will remain and continue with you all for your progress and joy in the faith so that your proud confidence in me may abound in Christ Jesus through my coming to you again*

Knowing, that His work was not yet finished, Paul pressed on, being absolutely sure that his labor would not be in vain. Paul, like many of us, had fleshly reasons for wanting to be with the Lord, yet he was willing to stay and serve on earth as long as the Lord required him, convinced the time would be fruitful and God would accomplish all He had ordained.

We too, should be willing to remain in the world as long as God has any work for us to do. Do we share Paul's confidence that God will use our lives to accomplish all He has ordained?

~~~

1:27 *Only conduct yourselves in a manner worthy of the gospel of Christ...*

Look up the verses below, and record their theme.

James 1:22-27

_____

_____

_____

_____

_____

_____

Colossians 4:6

_____

_____

_____

_____

_____

Matthew 5:13

_____

_____

_____

_____

_____

_____

1 Peter 1:17

_____

_____

_____

_____

_____

_____

How do these verses teach that we should live our lives? (Or, using Paul's words "conduct ourselves")

_____

_____

_____

_____

_____

_____

_____

_____

_____

_____

_____

Paul addresses our conduct both as our outward testimony" "*with one mind striving together for the faith of the gospel*' as well as with each other inside the church, "standing firm in one spirit". We should stand together in truth and in unity.

~~~

1:28 *in no way alarmed by your opponents*

Here Paul contrasts the saints and messengers of God with those opposed to the gospel of truth. It is clear that those opposed are on the road to perdition; and the saints walk the walk of salvation.

Is Paul encouraging or discouraging the Philippians who are being persecuted?

_____

We too, should not be discouraged when we are discriminated against or persecuted by enemies of the cross. We can take solace knowing that these persecutions are certain witnesses from God both of our salvation, and of the destruction of the wicked.

~~~

<u>Weekend Stop</u>

1:29-30 *For to you it has been granted for Christ's sake, not only to believe in Him, but also to suffer for His sake, experiencing the same conflict which you saw in me, and now hear to be in me*

Paul clearly states in verses 29 and 30 the reason for his encouragement. It should be noted that the Philippians were not suffering because they had done anything wrong, but were being persecuted because they professed Christ as Lord who died for them and rose again.

How often do you find an attitude with in our churches that if someone is suffering, they are simply being punished or disciplined for a sin?

_____

_____

_____

_____

Pondering Paul's exhortation, his own life, persecutions and witness along with the rest of the apostles, do you believe this attitude is accurate 100% of the time? Most of the time?

_____

_____

Read Matthew 7:2-3 below:

For in the way you judge, you will be judged; and by your standard of measure, it will be measured to you. Why do you look at the speck that is in your brother's eye, but do not notice the log that is in your own eye. "Or how can you say to your brother, 'Let me take the speck out of your eye,' and behold, the log is in your own eye? "You hypocrite, first take the log out of your own eye, and then you will see clearly to take the speck out of your brother's eye".

How do you think this applies to the situation
of judging within the church?

_____

_____

_____

_____

_____

_____

_____

_____

~~~

Week Two

Day One

2:1 *Therefore if there is any encouragement in Christ....*

In the first verse of chapter two, Paul exhorts the followers of Christ to giving proofs of their fervent love to each other. We should encourage each other as Christ encourages our own soul.

~~~

2:2 *make my joy complete by being of the same mind, maintaining the same love, united in spirit, intent on one purpose*

Here is the theme of unity in the church- one of the biggest weaknesses of our modern church.

In verse two, Paul gives four exhortations to the Philippians that would make his joy complete. What are they?

1._____

2._____

3._____

4._____

Paul further explains the heart of this
exhortation in verse three.

~~~

2:3 *Do nothing from selfishness or empty
conceit, but with humility of mind regard one
another as more important than yourselves;*

It seems as Paul is stating that it is possible to
do good things with a hard heart. He exhorts
against this and tells us that our actions are to
be done humbly, as he paraphrases the
'golden rule' for us.
Look up the Scripture References below and
write how they relate to this verse.
Romans 12:10

_____

_____

_____

John 13:34

_____

_____

_____

Leviticus 19:18

_____

_____

_____

~~~

2:4-5 *do not merely look out for your own
personal interests, but also for the interests of
others. Have this attitude in yourselves which
was also in Christ Jesus*
How hard this can be! Look up Jesus' words in
Matthew 5:39-45. Explain how Christ's words
in recorded in Matthew compliment Paul's
exhortation here in verses four and five.

_____

_____

_____

_____

_____

_____

_____

_____

~~~

<u>Day Two</u>

2:6-11 *Who, being in very nature God,*
did not consider equality with God something
to be grasped, but made himself nothing,
taking the very nature of a servant,
being made in human likeness.
And being found in appearance as a man,
he humbled himself and became obedient to
death— even death on a cross!
Therefore God exalted him to the highest place
and gave him the name that is above every
name, that at the name of Jesus every knee
should bow, in heaven and on earth and under
the earth, and every tongue confess that Jesus
Christ is Lord, to the glory of God the
Father.(NIV)

This beautiful doxology must be taken as a
whole, rather than broken up verse by verse.
Christ, the second person in the God-head,
knew that he might rightfully and lawfully not
appear in the base flesh of man, but remain
with majesty fit for God, yet he chose rather to
humble himself. Of his own will, he left the

glory he had with the Father before the world began. His life on earth displays one of His two states – the servant Christ who died a horrific death on the cross to atone for our sins. Yet, this is only one of His states.

Read Revelation 1:12-18 printed below and write the physical and spiritual attributes of Christ.

Then I turned to see the voice that was speaking with me. And having turned I saw seven golden lampstands; and in the middle of the lampstands I saw one like a son of man, clothed in a robe reaching to the feet, and girded across His chest with a golden sash. His head and His hair were white like white wool, like snow; and His eyes were like a flame of fire. His feet were like burnished bronze, when it has been made to glow in a furnace, and His voice was like the sound of many waters. In His right hand He held seven stars, and out of His mouth came a sharp two-edged sword; and His face was like the sun shining in its strength. When I saw Him, I fell at His feet like a dead man. And He placed His right hand on me, saying, "Do not be afraid; I am the first and the last, and the living One; and I was dead, and behold, I am alive forevermore, and I have the keys of death and of Hades.

_____

_____

_____

_____

_____

_____

_____

_____

_____

_____

_____

_____

_____

_____

_____

_____

_____

_____

_____

_____

_____

_____

_____

_____

_____

_____

_____

_____

_____

_____

We must remember that Jesus is no longer on the cross. He is no longer humbled or suffering. Rather, He sits exalted at the right hand of God until the Father makes His enemies a footstool for His feet. (Psalm 110)

~~~

2:12 *So then, my beloved, just as you have always obeyed, not as in my presence only, but now much more in my absence, work out your salvation with fear and trembling*

Paul joins this statement to his previous ones with the conjunctive 'So'(NASB) , or 'Therefore'(NIV). Paul is saying, therefore, because of these things I have told you, obey the Lord whether I am in your presence or not. Let whatever you do glorify God, whether it is behind closed doors, in the presence of other Christians, in the presence of your minister or in the presence of pagans.

How is our behavior when we are away from church? When we are stressed? In heavy traffic? In long grocery lines? With cranky children?

Then Paul tells the Philippians to '*work out your salvation with fear and trembling'*

This is a difficult part of the verse, and we'd best not avoid it. Let us "rightly divide" and correctly handle God's Word of truth.

Notice that Paul does not say to 'earn your salvation'. There is nothing we can do to earn our salvation. Let's pause here for a moment. Rewrite the following verses I your own words.
John 6:37

_____

_____

_____

_____

_____

_____

_____

Romans 8:29

_____

_____

_____

_____

_____

_____

Ephesians 1:4-7

_____

_____

_____

_____

_____

_____

_____

_____

_____

_____

_____

_____

We have determined that Paul is not saying
that we must earn our salvation by our walk,
so what does he mean 'work out your own
salvation?' There are many different
explanations of this verse found in
commentaries. I believe Paul is exhorting the
Philippians to do two things. 1) We experience
God's salvation in our lives on earth, but this is
lived out in eternity. Paul encourages the saints

to work obediently during their time (of salvation) on earth. 2) We grow up in our walk with God, or as Peter phrases it, "*like newborn babies, long for the pure milk of the word, so that by it you may grow in respect to salvation*" (1 Peter 2:2) As we grow we are learning the things of God, and putting Biblical concepts in our minds and hearts (internalizing them) and then we live them out (externalizing them).

Read the following verses and see if you come to the same conclusion, then state why or why not.

- Ephesians 2:10
- 1 Peter 1:17
- Philippians 1:5-6

_____

_____

_____

_____

_____

_____

_____

_____

_____

_____

_____

_____

We'll see if the next verse clarifies our answers
a bit.

~~~

Day Three

2:13 *for it is God who is at work in you, both to will and to work for His good pleasure*

According to this verse, <u>who</u> is at work in us?

_____

_____

Whose will and good pleasure does He accomplish?

_____

_____

Hallelujah! God works in us according to HIS good pleasure - Not for any merit of our own. It is God that works in us - Here is our encouragement and our promise. Though we do not will to do any good things by our own inborn nature, but we now do because God has made of our wicked will a good will!

~~~

2:14-15 *Do everything without complaining or arguing, so that you may become blameless*

and pure, children of God without fault in a
crooked and depraved generation, in which
you shine like stars in the universe. (NIV)

Let our conduct be pure and upright. Let us
conduct ourselves without grumbling and
complaining. In verse 2:15, Paul continues the
thought of 'working out your own salvation',
that is growing in our walk with God from
verse 13. As we grow in the Lord, He cleanses
our lives more and more. Our thoughts, actions
and life become more and more pure. This is
called <u>progressive sanctification</u>.

Read James 2:18 below:
But someone may well say, "You have faith
and I have works; show me your faith without
the works, and I will show you my faith by my
works."

Check the correct answer according to the text in James.

- ❑ Works produces salvation
- ❑ Works produces faith
- ❑ Faith produces works

The fruit of our faith is our deeds!

Ponder: Are our deeds pleasing to God? Have they become increasingly pleasing to God (more Scriptural) as we have lived out our Christian walk?

~~~

<u>Day Four</u>

2:16 *holding fast to the word of life...*
Some manuscripts say "holding out the word of life". We are surely to do both. God's Word is our life jacket and our hope that we cling to and offer to others.

We can trust God's promises!
What does God say about Himself in Malachi 3:6?

_____

_____

_____

_____

_____

_____

How does Hebrews 6:19-20 address our hope?

_____

_____

_____

_____

_____

_____

_____

What title does Christ give Himself in John
8:12?

_____

_____

_____

_____

_____

_____

Read Matthew 5:14-16. What does Christ call
believers in Matthew 5:14?

What does Jesus tell Christians that they
should do in Matthew 5:16?

_____

_____

_____

_____

_____

_____

_____

Clearly, our position of both holding fast to
God's Word as well as holding out God's Word
is a Biblical one.

~~~

Day Five

2:17-18 *But even if I am being poured out as a drink offering upon the sacrifice and service of your faith, I rejoice and share my joy with you all. You too, I urge you, rejoice in the same way and share your joy with me*

Paul makes a comparison to the Old Testament sacrifices – a comparison his audience would be familiar with. He says he is poured out as the drink offerings of wine or oil was, which was poured upon the sacrifice (here he calls it the sacrifice of their faith). Paul is willing to lay down his life for the sake of Christ, and his Gospel.

It is doubtful God has called us to make the same sacrifice as Paul, but should we be any less willing if He did?

~~~

2:19-22 *....I hope to send you Timothy shortly...for I have no one else who will be genuinely concerned...for they all seek after*

their own interests...he has served me like a
child serving his father...

Isn't it wonderful to share a ministry with
someone who has a like-heart? Notice who it is
Paul trusts, someone who seeks after Jesus
Christ's interests rather than his own. Timothy
serves under Paul faithfully as a child would
serve under his own father. It is also a
reminder to us that we, too, should be seeking
after Christ's interests above our own. This is
one of the things that makes us both
trustworthy and faithful stewards.

~~~

Weekend Stop

2:23-26 *Therefore I hope to send him immediately...but I thought it necessary to sent to you Epaphroditus because he was longing for you all and was distressed because you had heard that he was sick...*

Do we find this kind of longing in our church? Do we long to help those who are sick the was the Philippians must have longed to help Epaphroditus? When we are sick, do we long to comfort those that are distressed at our illness?

~~~

2:27-30 *For indeed he was sick to the point of death but God had mercy on him...therefore I have sent him all the more eagerly...receive him then in the Lord with all joy and hold men like him in high regard because he came close to death for the work of Christ...*

Paul gives us another flag as to how to receive ministers of the Word of God. Re-read verse

2:29 in your Bible. How does the text tell us to receive men like him? Why?

_____

_____

_____

_____

_____

_____

_____

_____

_____

~~~

Week Three

<u>Day One</u>

3:1 *Finally, my brethren, rejoice in the Lord. To write the same things again is no trouble to me, and it is a safeguard for you*

Paul penned the words of God as the Holy Spirit led him. Just as it is profitable for us to search God's Word daily and is a safeguard to us, it was also a safeguard to the Philippian church.

Read the verses below and record what they say about knowing God's Word.

2 Timothy 2:15

_____

_____

_____

_____

_____

Acts 17:11

_____

_____

_____

_____

_____

Deuteronomy 6:6-9

_____

_____

_____

_____

~~~

<u>Day Two</u>

3:2-3 ...*Beware of the false circumcision for we are the true circumcision, who worship in the Spirit of God and glory in Christ Jesus and put no confidence in the flesh.*

All those who were born Jewish are not automatically saved by their "Jewishness" or their heritage just as no one is saved simply by being born into a Christian family. The Bible is clear on what it means to be 'saved'.

Do you know anyone who believes they are saved because their parents are Christian and they were brought up in the church? How might you answer them?

~~~

3:4-7 ...*although I myself might have confidence even in the flesh. If anyone else has a mind to put confidence in the flesh, I far more: circumcised the eighth day, of the nation of Israel, of the tribe of Benjamin, a Hebrew of Hebrews; as to the Law, a Pharisee;*

as to zeal, a persecutor of the church; as to
the righteousness which is in the Law, found
blameless. But whatever things were gain to
me, those things I have counted as loss for the
sake of Christ.

Paul gives us a good answer to the ones who think they are saved because they were brought up in church, or their parents were Christian or their grandfather was a preacher.

Paul addresses this topic again in great detail in Galatians 4:21-31. After reading that section of text, come back and record your insights as to what Paul is saying and how that relates to Philippians 3:4-7.

_____

_____

_____

_____

_____

_____

_____

_____

_____

_____

_____

_____

_____

_____

_____

_____

_____

Paul makes a strong statement in verse 7
which he continues in verse 8. We will address
it below.

~~~

<u>Day Three</u>

3:8 *Yea doubtless, and I count all things but loss for the excellency of the knowledge of Christ Jesus my Lord: for whom I have suffered the loss of all things, and do count them but dung, that I may win Christ*
He counts all the status and advantages he had as a practicing Jew dung as compared to Christ and what he has in Christ.

Do you think Paul's life became harder or easier once he became a Christian?
Record Paul's experiences as a Christian as stated in 2 Corinthians 6:4-5:

_____

_____

_____

_____

_____

_____

2 Corinthians 11:23-27

_____

_____

_____

_____

_____

_____

_____

_____

_____

_____

_____

_____

Wow! We are now more fully understanding Paul's comment in Philippians 1:21, "*For to me, to live is Christ and to die is gain.*"

Though Paul fully understood the life and lifestyle and respect that he gave up, he fully embraced the temporal sufferings to walk the walk God called him to.

When hard times come in our lives, do we do the same?

<u>Day Four</u>

3:9-11 ...*and may be found in Him...that I may know Him..*

Paul reiterates the real Christian walk. The book of James emphasizes this too. A mere profession of faith is not enough. There is no magic prayer or words that give us "fire insurance". The Christian walk is detailed for us in these passages.

1. We have a righteousness through
   _____ which
   comes from God on the basis of
   _____. (Verse 9)

2. We have this so we may know Christ
   and the power of His
   _____ and the fellowship
   of His _____ being
   _____ to His death
   (Verse 10)

3. ...in order that we may attain to the
   _____ from
   the dead. (Verse 11)

This is our new life, attitude and walk in Christ!

~~~

<u>Day Five</u>

3:12 *Not that I have already obtained it or have already become perfect....*

Once we are saved, we are saved – so why do you think Paul says he has not already obtained it?

_____

_____

_____

_____

_____

The answer lies in the progressive sanctification we studied earlier. As we walk with God, God progressively cleanses our lives. Hebrews 10:14 reads, *For by one offering He [Christ] has perfected forever those who are <u>being</u> sanctified.* [NKJV]

We are justified by our salvation. This is a legal term, and gives our position before God. It is not "just as if I'd never sinned". It is as a guilty man goes before a judge because of his law breaking and a man pays his fine so he will not go to jail but walk free. Christ paid our fine, and we are justified legally before God. Sanctification is our purity before God. We are not made perfect the day we are saved. Yet, we read in Hebrews 10:10 *By this will we have been sanctified through the offering of the body of Jesus Christ once for all.* Is the Bible contradicting itself?

As Paul would say, "By no means!"

There is a degree of sanctification as we are made righteous through Christ's blood. Through Christ's sacrifice God will dwell with His elect through the Holy Spirit. As we walk with God, our lives become more and more sanctified as we become progressively conformed to Christ's image. Romans 12:1 gives us a vivid picture of a life dedicated to Christ. According to Romans 12:1, how should our lives be lived?

_____

_____

_____

_____

_____

We will never fully attain perfection on this side of eternity, but there is a visible progressive purity in the life and walk of a Christian.

~~~

3:13 *Not that I have already obtained it or have already become perfect, but I press on so that I may lay hold of that for which also I was laid hold of by Christ Jesus.*

Again, Paul has not yet been physically resurrected in his new body nor has he already been made perfect. Yet, he presses on the upward way. Read Paul's statements in Galatians 4:11 and 1 Thessalonians 3:5.

Does it seem to you that Paul was always aware of Christ and his own calling given by Christ?

I believe so, yet he clearly states that his labor was out of love for Christ and His people.

He states this at the beginning and ending of many of his letters including here in Philippians 1:3-4.

~~~

3:14-15 *I press toward the goal for the prize of the upward call of God in Christ Jesus. Therefore let us, as many as are mature, have this mind; and if in anything you think otherwise, God will reveal even this to you;* Paul finishes his thought from the previous verses and exhorts us to have the same attitude.

Two things we should note from these verses in chapter three. First, those who are not mature should be patiently waited for. Secondly, we need to judge the false teachers by their fruits. Notice that Paul does not hesitate to set forth himself as an example!

Can we as confidently put our own lives forth as an example and testimony to Christ?

~~~

3:16 *Nevertheless, to the degree that we have already attained, let us walk by the same rule, let us be of the same mind*

How do the following passages address this same subject?

Romans 12:10

_____

_____

_____

_____

_____

1 Corinthians 1:10

_____

_____

_____

_____

_____

~~~

3:17 *Brethren, join in following my example, and observe those who walk according to the pattern you have in us*

Based on the verses we have read, What pattern do you think Paul is speaking of?

_____

_____

_____

_____

_____

_____

_____

_____

_____

Paul clearly asks the Philippians to imitate him and those who follow his example. In the next verses, he will draw a strong distinction between those who live a godly life and those who don't.

~~~

3:18-19 *For many walk, of whom I often told you, and now tell you even weeping, that they are enemies of the cross of Christ whose end is destruction, whose god is their appetite, and whose glory is in their shame, who set their minds on earthly things.*

What is Paul's attitude toward the enemies of the cross? _____

It is striking that despite his persecutions from enemies of the cross, and despite the jeering and lack of respect he receives from them, his attitude is one of sorrow for them – not anger. He speaks of them in sorrow and tears.

How does our own attitude about enemies of the cross compare with Paul's?

_____

_____

_____

_____

_____

Do you think our inward attitude will affect our outward behavior?

_____

_____

_____

_____

_____

_____

~~~

3:20-21 *For our citizenship is in heaven, from which also we eagerly wait for a Savior, the Lord Jesus Christ who will transform the body of our humble state into conformity with the body of His glory, by the exertion of the power that He has even to subject all things to Himself*

Where is our citizenship? _____

Beloved, it is so easy to forget this and get entangled with the world's joys and sorrows and stresses.

This theme is addressed throughout the Bible. Study the following passages and record their emphasis and what they teach about our real home.

Ephesians 2:19

_____

_____

_____

_____

_____

_____

1 Peter 2:11

_____

_____

_____

Leviticus 25:23

_____

_____

_____

_____

_____

_____

Hebrews 11:9-10

_____

_____

_____

_____

_____

_____

Your thoughts:

_____

_____

_____

_____

_____

_____

The rest of the passage speaks of the power of
the sovereignty of Christ. It tells how we can
rest in Him knowing that He will transform our
bodies from their humble state to be in
conformity with His body of glory, by the
exertion of the power that He has even to
subject **all** things to Himself. Glory! What a
hope we have!

~~~

Week Four

<u>Day One</u>

4:1 *Therefore, my beloved brethren whom I long to see, my joy and crown, in this way stand firm in the Lord, my beloved*

Did you notice how affectionately Paul writes to the Philippian church?

What words does he use to express the tenderness and love of God he feels for them?

_____

_____

Verse 4:1 begins with a connecting clause "Therefore". Paul is saying, "Therefore, since you have of knowledge of these things, because of what I have written to you, use and practice what I have told you to stand firm in the Lord."

What are some of the ways Paul enumerates in chapter three that we might practice to stand firm in the Lord?

_____

_____

_____

_____

_____

_____

_____

_____

_____

_____

~~~

4:2 *I urge Euodia and I urge Syntyche to live in harmony in the Lord*

Here Paul urges two women, who were members of this church at Philippi, and at odds with each other to put aside their differences and live in harmony with each other.

Read Christ's words in Matthew 5:9. How do you think this verse relates to the blessing Jesus gave in Matthew?

_____

_____

_____

_____

_____

~~~

4:3 *Indeed, true companion, I ask you also to help these women who have shared my struggle in the cause of the gospel, together with Clement also and the rest of my fellow workers, whose names are in the book of life.* Who said Paul didn't recognize women?! Here he petitions that the church help the women who helped in the furtherance of the gospel as well as others who helped Paul in his ministry.

Do we also give those that serve in our churches the help and compensation they need?

~~~

4:4 *Rejoice in the Lord always...*
Paul seems to draw a distinction between the short-lived "joy" of the world and the true joy of a Christian. What the unsaved world actually experiences is happiness, which comes and goes based on circumstance. The Greek word

translated *rejoice* is chairō and it means to rejoice exceedingly, be glad, or thrive. Webster defines thrive as "To grow; to increase in bulk or stature; to flourish". We must grow and flourish in Christ Jesus.

~~~

<u>Day Two</u>

4:4 *Let your gentle spirit be known to all men.*
The Lord is near.

It is said that a picture is worth a thousand
words. This can also be said for our behavior.
Can you think of any examples where
someone's reputation because of behavior
went before them? How does someone's
behavior effect your first impression of them?

_____

_____

_____

_____

_____

_____

~~~

4:6-7 *Be anxious for nothing, but in everything*
by prayer and supplication with thanksgiving
*let your requests be made known to God. **And***
the peace of God, which surpasses all
comprehension, will guard your hearts and
your minds in Christ Jesus.

We are not to be anxious for anything, but with sure confidence give thanks to God and trust Him to provide whatever we have need of.

Read Matthew 6:25-34. What is the main subject of these passages?

_____

_____

What does Jesus tell us to do about it?

_____

_____

How do we carry out His command? (Verse 33)

_____

_____

Looking back at verse 7 in our chapter here, we see the connecting word 'and'. Verse 7 is thrown around the Christian community a lot as a blanket promise, but they are forgetting the connector 'and'. You may have noticed 'and' has been written in boldface type in our Scripture passage above. The promise in verse 7 is contingent on our behavior in verse 6.

When we are not anxious but in everything by prayer and supplication and thanks let our requests be known to God <u>then</u> the peace of God which surpasses all understanding will guard our hearts and minds in Christ Jesus. The text does not say "Do not be anxious about anything... but regardless, the peace of God will guard our hearts and minds..."
Paul's exhortation here rings of Isaiah 26:3. Please take a moment to read the verse above in Isaiah and write it on the lines below.

_____

_____

_____

_____

_____

Who does God say He will keep in perfect peace?

_____

_____

Why will God keep him in perfect peace? (It
tells us in Isaiah 26:3 following the word
because)

~~~

<u>Day Three</u>

4:8-9 *Finally, brethren, whatever is true, whatever is honorable, whatever is right, whatever is pure, whatever is lovely, whatever is of good repute, if there is any excellence and if anything worthy of praise, dwell on these things. The things you have learned and received and heard and seen in me, practice these things, and the God of peace will be with you.*

Verse 8 is one of my favorite passages! Paul gives us the 'formula' for having peace of mind. We dwell on the things of God. We count our blessings. There are so many blessings. It is easy when something goes wrong to focus on that. Physically, if we hurt part of our body, we tend to focus on the limb that is hurt rather than all the other limbs that feel good. Paul is telling us to do something that we are only capable of doing through the Holy Spirit that dwells in us. We can never have peace without God's Spirit, and we will never have His Spirit living in us unless we are saved. (John 14:23)

In the lines below, list the eight areas Paul exhorts us to dwell on.

1._____

2._____

3._____

4._____

5._____

6._____

7._____

8._____

Read Romans 14:19. Do you think that is a good summary of many of the things Paul addressed here in Philippians? Do you think Paul could be referring to these actions when he asks the church to practice the things they have learned from him? Why or why not?

_____

_____

_____

_____

_____

4:10 *But I rejoiced in the Lord greatly, that now at last you have revived your concern for me.....*

It is right to help a minister who is going through hard times. Just as James told us that "Faith without works is dead" (James 2:26), so Paul thanks the Philippians for not only *feeling* for him, but for doing something and *helping* him.

Is there anything in our lives we need to put feet on? That is, is there something or someone we have felt sorry for or empathy for that we need to help?

~~~

Day Four

4:11-12 *Not that I speak from want, for I have learned to be content in whatever circumstances I am. I know how to get along with humble means, and I also know how to live in prosperity; in any and every circumstance I have learned the secret of being filled and going hungry, both of having abundance and suffering need*

Paul has lived in prosperity and in poverty and need. He tells the church that he knows how to conduct himself in each, and how to dwell on the good and take out the good from all of them. In each of these states, he implies that he had learned the lesson perfectly, as mueō, the word translated 'learned' implies; he was thoroughly instructed in each area.

God cares more about our spiritual state then our comfort. Yet, humanly, I admit to wanting to be comfortable. I've learned that the longer I struggle in an uncomfortable situation the longer it takes for me to learn the lesson God is teaching me, and He will keep me there until

I learn it or bring it back into my life again a short time later. Have you noticed the same thing?

Paul gives us a wonderful example of the student of God we should strive to be!

~~~

4:13-14 *I can do all things through Him who strengthens me. Nevertheless, you have done well to share with me in my affliction*

Though Paul can do all things by the strength God gives him, he appreciates someone to share in his afflictions and lend a hand and heart of support. Isn't that what we all long for- someone to share our burdens with, and lend us both a shoulder and a helping hand?

~~~

4:15-17 *You yourselves also know, ... no church shared with me in the matter of giving and receiving but you alone; for even in Thessalonica you sent a gift more than once for my needs Not that I seek the gift itself, but I seek for the profit which increases to your account.*

What is Paul concerned about in these passages? The gift or the giver?

_____

How do you think this relates to our relationship with God? When He gives us blessings, or, we are waiting for His blessing, which should we concern ourselves with – the gift or the giver? _____

~~~

<u>Day Five</u>

4:18 *But I have received everything in full and have an abundance; I am amply supplied, having received from Epaphroditus what you have sent, a fragrant aroma, an acceptable sacrifice, well-pleasing to God.*

Paul refers to the offerings of the Philippians as *a fragrant aroma, an acceptable sacrifice, well-pleasing to God.*

What happened when God smelled the sweet savor of the sacrifice in Genesis 8:21?

_____

_____

_____

_____

How does Ephesians 5:2 refer to the sacrifice of Christ?

_____

_____

_____

_____

How does Revelation 5:8 refer to the prayers
of the saints?

_____

_____

_____

_____

1 Peter 2:5 speaks of how we should live our
lives. What instructions does it give?

_____

_____

_____

_____

~~~

Weekend Stop

4:19 *And my God will supply all your needs according to His riches in glory in Christ Jesus.* God provides for the spiritual needs of His children, according to the riches He has – and He owns all things! He gives all things richly to enjoy, bountifully and lavishly!

~~~

4:20-23 *Now to our God and Father be the glory forever and ever. Amen...The grace of the Lord Jesus Christ be with your spirit.*

According to James 1:17, where does every good and perfect gift come from?

_____

_____

Because all good things come from God, they are to be ascribed to his free grace and favor, and not because of any work of righteousness that man does.

In Matthew Henry's commentary of Philippians, he writes,

> "The apostle ends with praises to God. We should look upon God, under all our weakness and fears, not as an enemy, but as a Father, disposed to pity us and help us. We must give glory to God as a Father. God's grace and favour, which reconciled souls enjoy, with the whole of the graces in us, which flow from it, are all purchased for us by Christ's merit, and applied by his pleading for us; and therefore are justly called the grace of our Lord Jesus Christ."

As Paul leaves the church with a blessing, and we part ways, "May the grace of the Lord Jesus Christ also be with your spirit". May God bless you richly as you continue study in His Word!

Your concluding thoughts:

_____

_____

_____

_____

_____

_____

_____

_____

_____

_____

_____

_____

_____

_____

_____

_____

_____

_____

~~~